GODDESS OF MUNICH, GERMANY

CHEY CALISO

Content warning: domestic violence, intense alcohol and drug use,
child pornography, racism, mention of death

Main Characters:

Athena Katsopolis – The main protagonist of the story. She was born in Munich, Germany, and dreads life in America.

Nari Katsopolis – Athena's younger sister who she is very close to but at times, Athena admits she can get aggravated by her when she doesn't keep her mouth shut.

Min-Ji Katsopolis – Athena and Nari's mother. Wife to Vangelis.

Vangelis Katsopolis – Athena and Nari's father who is very overprotective of his girls. Husband to Min-ji.

Makena – Athena's best friend since seventh grade.

Amina – A close friend of Athena since she first came to the states. She is known as the friend that Athena loves to have fun with.

Giovanni Laterza – Athena's boyfriend who she has been having serious problems with.

Natalie – One of Giovanni's closest friends who Athena despises and admits she is jealous of.

1

I set my bottle of Jack Daniels on my wooden nightstand hoping I can fall asleep. I drank four gulps of it and still do not feel affected. It's now 4 a.m. I've never had this much anxiety in my life. My situation? I'm currently in an abusive relationship that I haven't opened up to anyone about, not even to Makena, who I've been best friends with since seventh grade.

His name is Giovanni. He's my first love and probably the only man I'll be in love with, but this relationship cannot last. He has sexually and physically abused me. I have scratches and bruises from the physical pain he has caused.

I want to break up with Giovanni so badly, but I feel like that is just going to make it even worse. Nari walked into my room when I changed into a different shirt yesterday. We don't have a lock on our doors except for the bathroom, and she never knocks, which pisses me off. She found two different bruises on my left arm. I had to beg that little rat not to tell anyone.

I hate the feeling of makeup on my skin. I only own two lipsticks and one mascara, but I would have to use makeup if the bruises or scratches were in a noticeable area, like my neck or hands. Then I would find my mom's makeup and cover it.

I always thought Giovanni and I would be together forever, but my thoughts changed a few weeks ago. I always told him he needed help and that I would find some way to provide the help, but he refused, and it made him angry that I brought it up. So I gave up.

He would bring up marriage frequently and say that we would get married after I graduated from college. It was exciting to think about and I was always looking forward to it, but these thoughts changed about two months ago.

I graduated from high school two days ago, and last night was my last straw with Giovanni. The situation was so little, but when this kind of stuff would happen, it would turn into a bigger deal later on.

We went out to dinner at a German restaurant, and the owners of the restaurant were German as well, so I spoke to them in our native language. Our waitress was very friendly; we even made small talk with each other since the place wasn't busy. As we were giggling about something her dad was doing back in the kitchen, Giovanni believed we were talking bad about him. He cleared his throat loudly, clenching his steak knife while cutting his half-eaten steak. The waitress awkwardly smiled and left to go back into the kitchen.

"Is there a problem?" I asked calmly, rubbing his hand.

"What were you talking about?" He aggressively took his hand away.

"Oh, well we were talking about her dad," I responded calmly.

"Her dad?"

"Yes, her dad."

"Didn't seem like it."

"Excuse me?"

"Maybe if you spoke in English, I wouldn't assume you would be talking bad about me." He rolled his eyes.

Giovanni's native language wasn't English either, so this behavior was even more off-putting coming from him. He came to the United States even later than I did, yet he's the one who has a problem with me speaking my native language.

I noticed that in his house, they speak in English. He does this because he wants to improve his grammar. The only person he has spoken to in his native language is his father. It didn't bother me at all and I also didn't assume he was talking bad about me like how he did at the restaurant last night. Maybe that's because I'm aware that the world doesn't revolve around me. His spoiled ass thinks differently.

My parents are planning to throw me a big party, but I'm honestly not in the mood. Before this all happened, I dreamed of having the best graduation party, and they agreed to give it to me, but I don't know how to tell them that I changed my mind due to the various questions they will be asking.

My mother unintentionally made it worse when she said she wanted me to wear the sparkly red dress she bought me last year.

It was a beautiful dress; it gave Jessica Rabbit vibes, except I didn't have the curves. It was my favorite dress until Damiano, Giovanni's brother, invited me to dinner for his birthday and Giovanni entered the family bathroom while I was washing my hands. The door was locked but he managed to open it with a quarter. That was one problem of his: never giving me privacy, when he needed the bathroom, he wouldn't wait for me, he would just open the door with what he could.

He wanted to do it right then and there, but I wasn't comfortable having sex in a public area. He lifted his hand under the slit of my dress, but I attempted to push it away.

"Babe, please—not now and not here." I calmly said.

"It will be quick, I promise." he bit his lip and continued.

"No!" I then tried to unlock the door.

He grabbed me by his waist and started grinding on me. He then aggressively kissed me on the lips. I tried to shout for help but he covered my mouth, smearing my power-matte-red lipstick around the bottom of my face. Once he stopped, I looked at him and started bawling my eyes out. With the expensive mascara he gifted me running down my face, he said I looked like someone from a horror movie.

"Wipe your face—you don't want to ruin my brother's birthday." Then he left.

I would've felt guilty if I'd thrown the fifty-dollar dress away so I took a plastic bag and hid it deep in my closet where I wouldn't see it every day. I'm thinking I could give it to Nari if it fits her one day, but if not, I can always sell it and give the money back to Mom. I can't do that for a long time though. If I do it now, she'll question me on why I wanted to sell it, and I'm not ready to tell her the reason.

Damiano was nothing like Giovanni. He was very kind to me and would even call out Giovanni's behavior that he knew of. Each time he would, Giovanni would just say the same thing to him— "Mind your fucking business, Damiano"—and would go in his room and lock the door.

My trauma didn't start with Giovanni. It started at ten years old when I came to America. I saw a teacher give birth right in front of me the first week here. I ran to the classroom next door so another teacher would be able to take her to the hospital, but it was too late by the time Mr. Hatso came. The baby died because it was premature, and we couldn't get her to the hospital in time. None of us knew she was pregnant because she just wasn't ready to announce it yet, as it had only been four months.

It happened on a Thursday. At the time, I assumed she had taken Friday off, but she never returned after that Thursday. All of the students were nosy, but the other teachers and staff told us not to bring it up after that, so none of us knows where she is or what she is doing in life now. I tried searching for her on Facebook and Instagram a few months ago, but nothing is there. She must have disappeared from social media as well.

When I first stepped foot in America, I hated it. To make it even worse, we resided in Ohio. It's cold, it's boring, and the people can be weird! Like, why do strangers have to talk to me in the grocery store? I'm just here to pick up my fruits and ice cream and then leave! This is the reason I switched to using Instacart.

The only reason we came here was my dad's stupid job. Five months later, he got fired from it, and it took him a good two months to find a job again. He wasn't too worried about it, but my mom was panicking. She thought her income alone couldn't support all four of us.

A combination of smoke and hot dogs was the first smell I remember from when I first came here. Right after we left the airport, we didn't even stop at our new house. We stopped at my dad's friend's house because they were having a bonfire. They had met through the internet through some sketchy website, supposedly for international business. Now that I think about it, for all we know, the man could have had dead bodies in his basement and given us their parts to eat.

At that time, Nari and I complained to Dad that we were tired while Mom was pissed and yelled at him in Korean, causing stares from the other people present at the bonfire. To make us stop complaining, Dad gave Nari part of his hot dog and me a big scoop of potato chips, but we still groaned about being there, so he eventually gave up and we went to our new house.

My first impression of the house was that I would need to take a while to get used to it.

Many people told me it was a nice-looking, cozy home, but something about it was very off to me. I think it was because I needed a reason to hate everything in America at the time. Now that I've lived here for eight years, I would say there are two things I like about America: how good the key lime pie is and how fun high school and college parties are.

We got our house for $230,400, but due to the current state of housing markets in America, it's worth a lot more now. Our house has three bathrooms and four bedrooms, with a basement, ground floor, and second floor. Our backyard is very small, but we are usually indoors, so it's not a big deal to us.

Very often, I have these dreams where I'm back at the old house, and in the dreams, I'm still living there so I wake up disappointed. Outside, the house was white surrounded by smaller trees and plants. Very often, Mom would water them outside. Inside, the walls were yellow except for the bathroom, which had a black wall. My mom liked the house in Ohio better because it's a lot bigger with a more modern design. Even though the house we currently live in has much better qualities, I still love the old house more, especially since I have better memories from Ohio.

Mom has worked two jobs for twelve years now. She works as a travel advisor and is also an interpreter for German and Korean, both of them remote jobs. She doesn't need to use German as much, compared to Korean.

When I first came here, I spoke and understood English with no problems, but people had problems with me because of my thick German accent. Whenever I would talk, people couldn't understand and would keep asking me to repeat my sentence which frustrated me to the point where I gave up and didn't want to talk to any English speakers anymore. They would be frustrated, too, because they never ended up knowing what I had to say.

By the time I was twelve, the heavy accent was gone but I still had an accent. People could tell I wasn't from here. Even if I had been born here, I just know they would have still assumed I was from somewhere else. When I was fifteen, my German accent went away.

I had so many friends back in Germany and lost contact with all of them once I moved.

Luckily, I remembered most of their names. When I was fourteen, I got on social media, so I looked them up, found twelve of them, and started talking to all of them again. In the United States, my friendships don't last as long. The only long-lasting friendship I see myself having is with Makena and I don't care who comes and goes as long as I have her.

I was born in Munich, Germany. My dad is ethnically Greek but also from Munich. My grandparents on his side were from Greece. His dad was from Athens and his mother was from Kalamáta. My mom is from Busan, South Korea. My great-grandfather from Athens was looked at as a hero for saving people from getting mauled by a loose lion. He was able to destroy it with his bare hands. I found the story hard to believe but Vati never lies.

I plan to go back to Munich a few years after I finish school, or I want to return at least by the time I'm twenty-five. When I was eleven, I asked Vati for the first time, "Are we going back to Munich?" and he responded, "I don't know." At twelve, I asked the same question and he said he didn't want to go back and neither did Mom. I've never had the chance to travel back. It's been eight years since I last saw home.

Home is described differently depending on who you ask. When I asked Makena about home, she said it was her house on Halo Drive because it was where her whole family would come together at the end of the day to be able to spend time with one another. I asked Keira and she said even though she lives with her parents and brothers, she felt most at home at her grandmother's house because she treated her better than everyone else in the family and made sure to always keep her safe.

My home was Germany. I'll admit, we've had a lot of problems there and still do, but I am just so used to the environment there and I've shared a lot of memories where I was happy. Who knows—maybe if I returned, it probably wouldn't be the same Germany that I knew.

When I was fifteen, I had dreams of living in New York City. My cousin currently lives there. She moved five years ago, and when we would talk, she would always tell me how much fun she had going out to delicious restaurants, partying, and going to shows with her friends. Then we visited her for the weekend. Mom bought herself, Nari, and me a plane ticket to New York City. My cousin lived in a small one-bedroom apartment for two thousand dollars a month. We had to make room for the three of us in the living room. Once we went back to the airport to wait on our flight back to Columbus, Mom asked, "Do you still want to live in New York City?" Definitely not. I don't do well with small spaces, but I'd love to visit again.

My dad loved the city of Athens so much, along with being so fascinated by Athena the goddess's story. Originally, my name was going to be Vanessa, a name they both agreed on, but three hours before I was born, my dad convinced Mom to name me after the goddess Athena because my dad admired that she was associated with wisdom and had hope that I would be a wise person too. My dad told me that Mom was pissed at him because she was in labor when he begged her to agree on the name. Out of frustration, she automatically said yes.

Mom thought naming me Athena because of his reason was tacky at first then she eventually grew into it, but just for that, in order to get even, my mom chose my little sister's name even if my dad didn't agree with it. She chose Nari, a Korean name that means "lily." He didn't hate or like the name—it was kind of like "ehhh" for him.

My dad came from the Greek Orthodox faith, but his parents would read stories to him as a child about different Greek gods and goddesses growing up, and that's how his interest in Athena, Zeus, and Poseidon started.

I love both of the cultures I come from equally, but I feel like I barely know anything about Korean culture. I don't speak Korean and I do not understand any of it. With Greek, I understand numbers and greetings. I've been to Athens a few times.

When I was twelve, I considered living there and said I would become fluent in Greek by the time I was eighteen but that clearly didn't happen. I want to know more about Korean culture, but my mom doesn't want to tell me much. The only thing I know about Korean culture is food.

I eat Korean food a lot. I like it better than Greek and German food, actually. My favorites are fish cakes and kimchi, but my mom is so busy I don't have it as often as the Greek cuisine my dad always makes for Nari and I. Nari likes Greek food the most. Her favorite is Soutzoukakia which are basically just Greek meatballs. She used to fuck up saying the actual cuisine name, which annoyed Dad, so he would just say, "Honey, please just say Greek meatballs."

My Mom is an atheist and she raised Nari and me as Atheists as well. As a child, my dad would make the three of us go to this Greek Orthodox church with our grandparents. My mom would get so bored, she'd end up playing games on her phone, which resulted in them arguing once we got into the car.

"Min-ji, how disrespectful can you be? In front of my parents too?" Dad shouted.

"Honey, it's not my fault I get bored!"

"I do things for you. Why don't you take time out of your weekend to do something for me?!"

"Because I just told you, I get bored! At least I came!"

My mom and I hated my grandfather on my dad's side. He was super racist towards us. I had no idea what he was saying but Dad told me. He only spoke Greek and I always assumed something bad would come out of his mouth, so I always responded in German or English with something nasty back. "Shut the fuck up! You look like a clown!" "I hope grandma ends up leaving your stupid ass." "Do you want to see Satan, you old bitch?"

Another thing I hated about him was that he was disrespectful to my grandma. She would feel ashamed and worthless because of the harsh comments he would make towards her in front of everyone. We don't have to deal with Grandpa anymore because he's now six feet under. Mom and I weren't planning on going to his funeral at first, but Dad forced us. People knew we clearly didn't want to be there when I started going on my phone scrolling through Instagram and my mom was on her phone editing her selfies on the Perfect 365 app.

Mom comes into my room with a huge plate with some cut-up fruit. She comes in unexpectedly, so I didn't have time to hide the Jack Daniels. She just looks at it and shakes her head in disappointment.

"Oh Athena . . ." she says.

"Uhhhh . . ."

"Nari told me what happened." She sits down on my rocking chair and places the fruit on the table.

"What are you talking about?" I know what she is talking about. I don't even know why I ask. "That . . . Giovanni's not been good to you."

"I've been struggling to tell people, Mom. I promise I wanted to tell you, but I'm scared. If I tell you, it's only going to make it worse." I start bawling my eyes out.

"No Athena, if you don't tell a trusted adult, it will get worse. I never told anyone this but I almost got killed, so I had to leave Busan. Everyone thinks I left for work, but I left because I was scared to face him ever again."

"Who?"

"My ex-husband. His name was Dae-Jung. Our relationship started great. He was good to me, bought me gifts, and took very good care of me—fed me well, too. He was the best cook. Then, four years into our marriage, he was introduced to gambling and drugs by a close friend of his. I tried to get him to stop. I remember I flushed cocaine down the toilet, and he punched me so hard, it dislocated my jaw."

"Oh my . . . I'm so sorry, mom." I start crying even harder.

"It's okay Athena. My story gets worse though. After that, I still stayed with him. At one point he even held a knife to my throat so I wouldn't tell anyone his situation. I knew that if I stayed with him any longer, he would kill me. So I got a plane ticket to Germany as soon as I could, taking only what I could carry. So I had two suitcases and a backpack, and then I was headed for Germany. Not even Dad knows about this."

"I'm glad you're doing better now."

"Yeah. . . . A lot more happened, but I don't want to scare you too much. I'm just trying to let you know that if you don't leave right now, you'll be in a situation like mine. I haven't seen my mom physically in over twenty years. I miss her every day, and I hope that you and Nari can meet her in person one day too. She's a great woman."

I've only seen my Grandma on video chat. She's adorable. She loves cats, and always wears cat-printed clothing. For my sixteenth birthday, she gifted me her favorite cat sweater after finding the same one in the store in my size. She also gave me a jumbo Pompompurin plushy since she knew I was more of a dog person. One day I hope to have a Rottweiler. My mom hates having animals since the dog she was so attached to died back in Busan. Now, no pets are allowed to step foot in our house. She will never get over the pain. She even cried for three months straight.

My grandpa from my mom's side was never in the picture. He left my grandma, my mom, and my two uncles when they were very young and went to Sweden and met a new woman. I have no idea why. She was mid. My grandma was heartbroken but was ultimately okay because she still had her children. After I heard Mom tell that story, I felt really bad; she seemed like such a nice lady.

Unfortunately, since my grandma can't speak English and I can't speak Korean, my mom has to translate everything we say. My mom speaks Korean, English, and German. For a year, she went to school in the Philippines to learn English and then went back to South Korea and kept learning through the internet. She said it took her the longest to learn German, which she learned in three years.

When my mom was in the Philippines, the biggest cultural difference for her was getting in the tricycles. She was always used to taking the bus in Seoul and Busan. She mainly lived in Busan but did work in Seoul for about a year.

While in Seoul and the Philippines, she would party almost every night. While in Busan and Germany, she did not do as much but she still did go out at least once a week. When she first came to Germany, during the first week, she wanted to celebrate her escape from her ex, so she went to strip clubs and bars to party. She went alone at first and then met more people and eventually became friends with them. Finding out my mom was a party girl was low-key disturbing. She even told me she slept with her ex-husband's cousin when they met at a bar and went back to her place. This was a few years before she met her ex-husband. When he found out, he got pissed and slammed the table while she was eating.

She went with her four friends to learn English in the Philippines. They would go out every night and forget that they were not there to party but instead to prioritize schooling. Her two friends gave up on it and decided to go back to South Korea, but my mom and her other friend stayed and eventually learned during the year they were there. She said it was very easy for her to learn English, although her other friends who learned or at least attempted to learn English said they had a hard time with it.

Apparently, it's very hard to learn German. I wouldn't know because it's my native language. I remember I was a tutor in my sophomore year of high school for students who were taking German classes. Every student I've tutored frustrated me, so I gave up and stopped tutoring students after two weeks. I don't even know why I agreed to do it, as I wasn't even getting paid.

I started learning English at three years old, so I never struggled with communicating with people in the United States because I was already fluent by the time I came here.

I never understood why people were so surprised to know I was from Germany. Many Americans lack the understanding that being from a certain place doesn't automatically mean you also have that background. It's actually kind of funny, because these were the white Americans who had that logic.

"Where are you from?" asked some random kid from school.

"I'm from Germany. I came here at ten," I responded.

"Wait, really? You must be joking."

"No, why would I lie about my place of birth?" I responded with a resting bitch face.

"I don't know. I guess I've never seen a German person who looks like you."

"Like me?" I raised an eyebrow.

"So was your grandpa a Nazi?" He switched the subject. "You're fucking joking, right?"

"No, I want to know."

I didn't respond to his question. I had no time to educate people's ignorance and stupid jokes. My family wasn't even there during that time.

I remember another girl who also joked like that as well. She had once seen me coming out of my mom's car. As I was going to walk past her, she asked me "Wow, where did you get that sick Nazimobile?"

I responded with, "Excuse me bitch?" and she started to get a little intimidated by me when I gave that response.

"Uhhh . . ."

"Uhh, what?" I responded with an attitude.

"It was just a joke." She smiled nervously.

"Explain it to me then." I came closer.

"Well, 'cause your mom has a Volkswagen. It's also a nice car, by the way; I didn't mean to come across as offensive. I'm sorry," she said quickly.

"Don't ever say that shit to me again. I'm the wrong person to joke about shit like that, bitch. No wonder why you have no friends." I said, and then walked away while she ended up going to the bathroom to cry.

She was some girl from Franklin who was raised on a farm. Her dad died of a heart attack so her mother sold the farm and moved to Columbus. A lot of the girls thought she was weird and would walk away from her when she wanted to talk to them. I felt bad for her until one day a group of girls let her sit with them at lunch, and she made a crude joke about Indigenous Americans and it made the girls uncomfortable. They all looked at each other, got up at the same time, and went to the gym to watch the boys play basketball.

The comments they made annoyed me. It's okay, though, because I decided I wanted to start lying. After all, being honest all the time was getting boring.

My first victim was the ignorant guy. I told him I spoke a total of six languages: English, German, French, Spanish, Korean, and Dutch. I told him that I learned French by living in France for three years, that I learned Dutch by living in The Netherlands for two years, and the rest I taught myself. With my apparent knowledge of all of these languages, I told him I could tutor him in French since he needed the help for class. During our tutoring sessions, I ended up having him take notes of popular phrases which were actually all gibberish, so he ended up getting an F on the test. He only got one question right out of twenty-five.

Another thing I lied about was that I owned a St. Bernard named Toby. The girl loved dogs, probably because they were the only ones willing to be friends with her. I showed her a random picture of a dog I led her to believe was mine. I had found it on page six of Google, a.k.a. a watered-down version of the dark web.

I told her that I would get her one if she paid me six hundred dollars and we had a deal.

I went to the Amish to find a St. Bernard puppy and I asked for the most malicious one they had. The guy was confused but then led me to a puppy and said, "We don't have any mean dogs, but this little guy is only harmful when you carry him. He bites, growls, and shits uncontrollably when you feed him too much ice cream." I responded with, "Good enough. How much?" "One hundred fifty." I then took him to the girl's house and asked for my six hundred. I counted it all and then unlocked the back door to give her the puppy. As I was pulling out of her drive, I couldn't stop laughing.

The next day at school, I noticed a revolting tooth mark on her arm. Moral of the story: DO NOT FUCK WITH ME YOU TRIFLING CUNTS!

2

"I'm in love with you, Athena Katsopolis." This was how he first told me he loved me. We were at Hocking Hills with his friends. That day was so tiring because we went on a two-mile hike in 80-degree weather.

Once everyone showered, they went to play Just Dance but I was too tired. Natalie wanted me to join her. I wasn't feeling generous nor was I getting anything out of it, so I went to Gio's and my room for the night.

I went into the room we were staying in and read manga until I was ready to fall asleep.

Manga isn't my thing but *Death Note* is good.

I heard the door creak while I was on the verge of falling asleep. He laid next to me and whispered it in my ear. I was shocked. I didn't feel that way just yet, so I pretended I was asleep.

The following Friday, he took me out on a date. We went out to get ice cream in the best dessert place in Columbus. I got coconut while he got chocolate chip cookie dough. We took cute photos of ourselves on our date, staying there for about half an hour. I could tell that some people thought we were being gross as we were being lovey-dovey but I didn't notice anyone looking at me until Gio laughed and was like, "Did you see that bitter old bitch staring at us when we were hugging?"

Once we got back in the car, I knew I was finally ready. I told him I loved him. "Really?" he asked with a big smile.

"Yes, really," I responded.

"I love you so much, Athena."

We went to his house afterward. His grandma on his dad's side called him. They would talk about three times a month. They are pretty close. I said hi to her and she said that it would be lovely if we could meet one day.

Once the call ended, he then talked about taking a trip to Italy to meet his extended family. It would be nice to see Italy but I'd have to deal with meeting everyone. Ew. All thirty-three of them and counting.

The countries I've traveled to are Costa Rica, the Dominican Republic, Egypt, Australia, Ireland, and Greece. I loved Greece the most, especially Athens. The vibe, the art, and don't even get me started on the scenery. The scenery was so beautiful I had to take pictures everywhere we walked. I spammed my Instagram with these photos of Greece that annoyed a few people, so they ended up unfollowing me.

My favorite memory from Greece was going to the wedding of a couple who we had met just two days prior. When we were at the airport heading to Athens, a man from Greece was talking to our family. After a good conversation my parents had with him and his wife, they decided to invite us to the wedding. It was mainly so his fiancée from Minnesota, who had no one else to befriend, could have someone to talk to at her wedding. They seemed to have had the perfect wedding and were so happy that day. We kept in touch with them through Facebook and Instagram, but after three years, I noticed she had deleted her social media, and then a week later, my dad got a call from the man saying she recently had become extremely depressed because she missed her family and friends in Minnesota and she wasn't making any friends in Greece. He had found her in the tub when he came home from work and noticed a blade on the bathroom sink. She bled out and the whole tub was filled with water and blood mixed in. Her head was underwater as well. When my dad found out, he felt very sorry for him. My dad decided to ship him flowers. I remember the shipping being expensive.

Athens, Ohio? Now that was a different story. I went because there was a party going on at Ohio University, where Damiano attended. We went to two parties and they were really fun, it would have been the best time I'd ever had if Giovanni hadn't been there. The following Sunday, I assumed we were going home, but no, they wanted to explore Athens, Ohio. As someone who has traveled the world, Athens, Ohio, wasn't really exciting. Hell, even Ohio in general is boring.

I was hungover and if Giovanni's driving had gotten any worse, I would have puked on him. Now that I'm thinking about it, I should have decided to drink even more the night before and then I could have actually puked on him. He always has this habit of pressing on the break when it isn't necessary. Once in a while, when he is driving and does it, I will tell him to get out of the driver's seat and let me drive. He drives a 2023 Mercedes-Benz. It's mid but he believes it's the best-looking car. I personally think my 2019 Toyota Corolla is better. Mercedes are nice cars too, but he chose the ugly one.

One time, a while after this, he was driving while I was in the back seat. He ended up getting lost and we ended up in some sketchy area. I remember locking the doors in the back and saying, "Thankfully, I'm not named after this Athens."

All the sightseeing we did took the whole day, so he decided he didn't want to go home that night, even though we had school in the morning. I don't even know why they wanted to sightsee; nothing was exciting in this city except partying. Maybe the basic nature excited them, but not me. As you can tell, they don't travel as much as I have. It's kind of interesting because throughout their whole lives, they could have traveled to anywhere they wanted, yet they've only been to Italy, the United States, and Costa Rica. They've had options to go to more places but declined for reasons I don't know of. They are just boring, rich people, I assume.

We stayed at Damiano's dorm that night and seven other people were sleeping over, too. We slept on the cold-ass floor with a thin-ass pink blanket that belonged to Damiano's ex. She cheated on him, and he never allowed her to pick up her stuff, so now it was a blanket for the guests.

Some random girl at, like, 3 a.m. started spooning me, so I pushed her away. I was so disgusted because once that happened, I was fully awake and couldn't go back to sleep. Then I noticed a dried-up "yogurt stain" on the blanket, around where my leg was. Witnessing that was the last straw for me.

"Giovanni . . . Giovanni . . ." I kept shaking him until he woke up. "What?!"

"If you don't get your ass up right now, I'm taking your car and leaving this place without you."

He was so mad at me for disrupting his beauty sleep but I didn't care anymore. We were so pissed at each other I didn't want to talk to him. He kept calling my name and I kept ignoring him. He then grabbed my wrist and squeezed it so tight. I tried to move my wrist but he kept squeezing it tighter, which I didn't think was possible.

"Let go of me!" I screamed in pain.

"Then stop fucking ignoring me."

"Okay!" He then smacked my wrist on the center console.

"Ow!"

"It's what you fucking deserved."

I had so much to say to him, but I was scared of more consequences. Sometimes I wonder how different he would have treated me if he hadn't had such a bad childhood. I always gained sympathy for him when he would remind me of how much trauma he endured as a child, and that's my problem.

I let him do this to me and I always took care of him because I love him, or, at, least loved him. I was starting to realize how much pain he gave me physically and mentally, so the love is starting to finally turn into hate.

The first red flag that I didn't pay attention to was when we were in the talking stage, and we got into the conversation of talking about our past. He asked if I was a virgin and I admitted I wasn't. His facial expression went from smiling to a deadpan face. He then wanted to know everything about that night. Who he was, what did he look like, and where had it taken place.

I didn't like talking about it, especially since we had only known each other for less than a week, so I kept it vague. I told him that I couldn't remember as much as I could, but I remembered that night vividly, and I mean vividly.

I was fifteen and went to Greece with my family. At Agia Anna Beach, I met a boy named Tobias, who was sixteen years old at the time. We exchanged our Snapchats, and he texted me later that night. I invited him to my Airbnb. I was sleeping in the same room as Nari but then snuck into the living room just for some dick. Worth it, though; he knew what he was doing.

We were at Makena's house one night having a game night involving drinks with four other people from school. The first game we played was Truth or Drink and a girl named Haley picked up a question and asked, "Who did you lose your virginity to? Describe them in heavy detail." After already taking three shots prior, along with drinking a Bud Light, I answered the question by saying, "He was named Tobias and I was convinced he was this sexy Greek god whose hands were sculpted by Aphrodite herself, bro!" We all laughed obnoxiously.

Once I realized Giovanni was listening, I then said, "Actually, now looking back, he wasn't even that cute . . ."

"Oh, shut up! You're probably still into him!" He then left.

Not at all. I mean, he was a cutie, but after that night, I kind of forgot about him, maybe because I didn't prioritize boys in my life back then. When I returned to the United States from Greece, he texted me two weeks later, but I never responded. He only asked for "pics" anyway. I'm not the type to send that kind of stuff. I'm not trying to risk my body being leaked. Gio even asked once, but I wasn't comfortable.

I then met Malik, someone from school who I wanted to mess around with for a couple of days. I knew he was attracted to me when he messaged heart eyes on my mirror selfie that I posted on my Instagram story. I figured I had nothing to lose so I straight up asked him, "Do you want to grab coffee?" when I saw him by himself at his locker. We got iced coffee, studied for our chemistry test at the coffee shop for about an hour, and then we went back to his place. This was a few months before Giovanni and I started talking.

After game night, I didn't want Gio to know more about my sexual past, but he eventually found out because, around our school, everyone talks about everyone. This is why I hated high school. He found out from Britney the blabber, so I was in trouble. When I found out she had snitched, I grabbed her by her braid, knocked her down, and left as if nothing happened.

Giovanni took his anger out on both Malik and I. Giovanni started roasting him in the hallways at school and then even called me out, saying, "Why would you sleep with him?! He's shaped like a stick!"

I told him to stop, and I apologized to Malik. Malik didn't blame me for his behavior, thankfully. He was aware of how crazy Giovanni was. He never liked the popular kids, and I don't either—too fake, too crazy, or just always making fun of someone.

I told Giovanni to stop messing with him, but I don't know why I tried; he would never listen to me anyway. I gave up telling him to stop, so all I said was that he was going to regret it.

He said it was cruel to bully people for how they looked and would call others out if someone made fun of someone's looks, but he would do the same thing when he was angry at someone. I called him out on that, but he just said that since he was furious with them, it was excusable.

He ended up getting suspended for threatening and bullying Malik. When Giovanni told me he got suspended, I responded with, "Well maybe you shouldn't mess with the principal's nephew." He then screamed at the top of his lungs "SHUT . . . THE . . . FUCK . . . UP . . ." I then hung up the phone and went to bed.

The following Saturday, he texted to ask if I wanted to come over but I said I had plans with my family. In reality, I was on my way to Oxford, Ohio, to party at Miami University. He kept asking how my family was and if I was having fun while I was drunk, and I tried my best to give him sober responses and he believed them. Sucker.

My childhood friend, Amina, who was older than me, attended Miami University and invited me to a Halloween party with her and the friends she had made at school. It was the first and last time I experimented with cocaine. I also had three shots of vodka and ended up blacking out. I woke up the next morning on her friend's couch.

Amina told me everything that had happened. Since her apartment was thirteen minutes away, she thought it was too far to carry me, so we went to crash at her friend's house that was only three minutes away. It was harder for her to carry me because she was wearing high heels—she was Daphne while I was Velma.

I woke up that morning hungover, with Giovanni spamming my phone with texts asking where I was. I was going to tell him the truth through text until he started calling me. He had set the photo for his contact photo as a picture of himself during prom night and that triggered a memory.

He had asked me to prom and I said yes. I was most excited about picking out a dress.

While going shopping, I loved this blue sequin gown, but he said no and picked out a red satin corset-style dress that I hated.

"I fucking hate it!" I shouted in the store, acting like a little kid. I'm not proud of that moment, by the way.

"Too bad. I decided we are going with red for prom, and that's final."

"No, I want blue!"

"Well, Natalie and Juan are doing blue for prom."

"Fuck her! What difference does it make if we have the same colors? Will she cry that I will look better?"

"Athena, take the dress off and give this dress to the fucking cashier."

"I hate you." I stormed back into the dressing room.

He bought the dress for me, but I went online to find the exact dress I wanted, and I was so happy they had it. I ordered the dress without telling him and showed up in the dress I liked.

He kept saying, "Wow," not because I looked good but because he was surprised that I was brave enough to disobey his orders. The only time we were together was when our moms were taking photos in his backyard. In the limo, I ended up sitting next to Travis and got to know his date. At prom, we sat at different tables, hung out with our friend groups, and rode home with other people.

"You made me look like a fucking idiot, bitch," was the first thing he said when we saw each other at school the next week.

"You knew I liked this dress better," I responded trying not to cry.

"I would have compromised and bought you another dress if you wanted, but only if it was red, because we were supposed to wear red," he said.

"Well, I wanted to pick out my outfit this time. During Halloween, you already chose to have us dress up as Hugh Hefner and the Playboy bunny. I didn't even want to dress up like that because I'm a minor, so I'm not comfortable wearing that!"

"Well, I made you wear it because I knew you would look good, and every girl was jealous of how fucking amazing you looked."

"I don't care about any other person's opinion!"

"Well, you should care. Sometimes stuff you pick out can be whack."

"I bet Tobias would have thought it looked good on me."

Giovanni slammed on the brakes and I ended up hitting my forehead on the dashboard. Jesus Christ, that hurt. I remember there were cars behind us that almost collided with us, but I didn't see the near misses; I just heard the cars honking behind us.

With that awful memory being brought up, I decided to lie about where I was. If I wasn't cheating on him then it was okay to lie. He bought it because if he ever did find out I was going out without him and lying about it, he would have beaten my ass, again.

We were both toxic in our own way. I'm not proud of it, but I've only done petty stuff since he started hitting me. The first six months of dating went well. We never argued, and he did little stuff to make me happy. His problem was that he was always clingy. I wasn't like that, but I dealt with it during that time. I then admitted there are times when I need space, especially coming home from work due to exhaustion. But he suspected it was because I needed to get away from him so I could cheat, so he would start disrespecting those boundaries.

I never cheated on him and I would never. The reason why he got so suspicious was because he lost trust in all women when he found out his ex, who he dated for four months, was still fucking her ex the whole time they were dating. I wasn't aware that he had healing to do until the second time he hit me and admitted that was the case.

I used to blame her for the pain Giovanni would give me, but I realized that this is on Giovanni now. I mean, I don't like the girl; she was a cheater, but I can't blame her when Giovanni is the problem here. He shouldn't have gotten into a relationship with me if he wasn't completely over her.

The reason why he's so clingy is because of child neglect. His dad wasn't involved in his life, while his mother was always busy because she's, like, some big fashion designer, I guess.

Everyone, especially in Ohio, buys her clothes, but to me, they're mid as fuck. I remember she offered to give me a blouse that looked like it came from the set of *Shake It Up*. Originally, it was $315, but I made an excuse saying I had too many clothes already.

"Wowwww. This apparel is lovely . . . and I appreciate the offer, Mrs. Laterza, but I have way too many clothes in my closet already. Thank you, though." I put on a fake smile.

Even though her clothes are horrible, I will admit that her make-up line is very good. It just came out a month ago. Giovanni gave me her expensive makeup for free, but since I don't like makeup, I only use the ones to help cover the bruises. I remember Giovanni was looking in his mom's closet and giving me the pink lipstick I liked from her brand, and while I was sitting on her bed, I scooted up and was sitting on something hard. I felt what it was, and then untucked the bed to see what it was, and then I revealed her warm, hot-pink-plastic dildo. I freaked out and threw it to the side of the room right when Giovanni came out, hitting him in the face. I was more traumatized that it was warm.

Giovanni's mom has strawberry blonde hair, wears reddish-orange lipstick most of the time, smells heavily of Gucci perfume, and has more wrinkles than average for someone her age. She gets it from smoking all the time and from the stress from her hard work. Giovanni wants her to quit smoking, but she just tells him to mind his business and then lights up a cigarette each time.

I don't smoke anymore but I have in the past. I remember going to a picnic for school. I got annoyed with everyone there, so I decided to go smoke by the lake. It was one of my teacher's cigarettes. I noticed a pack of Marlboro cigarettes in her Vera Bradley bag. When she went to the bathroom, I stole one and went to the bench right on the lake. As I was assuming I was going to be at peace, Natalie decided to come and bother me.

"I know you don't like me." She popped out of nowhere.

"Okay . . . and?" I responded with an attitude.

"But I want to know you more . . ."

"I don't care for you, Natalie. Listen to me when I say this. I don't like you and will never fucking like you," I said as the smoke got into her eyes.

"But what did I do to you?"

"You're racist to me, and you make fun of every girl just for male attention. But you have pretty eyes, I'll give you that."

"I'm sorry. I am." She looked down.

"I don't care for an apology. Apologize to all of those girls you've hurt, you 'pick me'-ass bitch." I then got up and walked away.

I never actually bought cigarettes myself. Other times I would usually steal them from Giovanni's mother. She had so many packs around the house, it wasn't like she was going to notice one was gone. The brand was Camel Blue. I took a pack when Giovanni was showering in his mother's bathroom, and I was lying on her bed. There was one on her nightstand and then three more in the drawer. I took one that was in the drawer and put it in my purse.

Giovanni found out that I stole them when he was taking me home from a party. I was super drunk while he had only had one drink. He took me back home, carried me up to my room, and put me in my bed, covering me with my comforter. He then left my house when I was already asleep, but I woke up the next morning with the cigarettes scattered all over my bed.

He probably found them when he was carrying me and felt a weird substance in my back pocket. I remember the pack with only two in it to my left, while the other ones were scattered within my comforter and a few outside of it. He never brought it up to me, so I pretended to forget.

Giovanni hates it when his mom and I smoke. He lectured me about it the first time he saw me do it so I just stopped smoking in front of him. He hates it because his favorite uncle on his father's side smoked to the point where he got lung cancer and died when Giovanni was ten years old. He still has photos with him around his room. He went to his funeral and the open casket gave him nightmares. It was the first dead body he saw, and while standing in front of the body, he thought that his uncle was going to open his eyes and shift his head towards him. Luckily, that didn't happen. He couldn't sleep for weeks after seeing him in that condition, so he asked to sleep in Damiano's bed with him but Damiano told him to "get lost" so he just ended up sleeping in his mom's bed. He didn't want to, but it was his last resort. Before they went to bed together, he would see a pack of cigarettes on the nightstand. He cried himself to sleep each time.

His mother is rich as fuck. I don't even know why she lives here in Columbus, Ohio.

Giovanni and Damiano never had to work jobs, while I've had three jobs so far in my life, and I'm only eighteen. Each month, their mother gives them a thousand dollars for their allowance. He spends a lot of that on me even when I told him not to, but he always spends money on me anyway. It's one of the reasons why I have dealt with his abuse for so long. I just ended up feeling guilty every time he bought me a gift, even though he would hit me prior to giving it to me.

He also was very loyal to me. He would describe how many men would be in serious relationships but still give attention to other women, but he would always tell me he wasn't like that and that if I did leave him, then it would be hard to find a man who is as loyal as him. I know he is loyal and it's a good quality to have in a relationship, but he just has so many other flaws to work on. I suggested therapy to him a few times, but he thinks he doesn't need it at all. He thinks he is perfect, along with his mother, but Damiano and I 100% disagree and believe that he needs help.

Damiano and I did bring it up one time while we were in his room, and he became so infuriated that he started slamming his desk and ripping the posters off his wall, telling us that he was completely fine. Okay, buddy.

That concerned me, and with Damiano not having seen this side of him before, he didn't know how to help him. I was frightened, so I ended up running out of the room and leaving his house. A lot of times when I would run from him, he would chase after me, but Damiano held him back and he couldn't catch up to me.

3

Giovanni first came to the United States when he was fifteen years old and a sophomore. I remember the first day he came to this school. It was during January, when I was a freshman. Every girl was talking about how hot he was and saying that they wanted to hook up with him in the bathroom. I don't know why; those bathrooms were crusty and always smelled like mac and cheese.

On his first day here, he asked me slowly where Mrs. Winjenfuratski's class was, and for a second I had no idea who he was talking about. Then I realized it was because we always call her "Mrs. W," because who can say that name without having a stroke?

Mrs. W was the chemistry teacher and her class wasn't that far from where I was going, so I walked him to her classroom and said thanks, expecting it to be the first and last time we would interact. The whole time we were with each other, I noticed him non-stop staring and smiling at me.

I didn't think anything of it and assumed that maybe it was an Italian thing. I don't know—I never really knew anything about Italian culture except for pizza, and I don't even like pizza, so what was the point in caring? I'm just kidding.

I think I hate pizza because my grandmother would bring us her pizza leftovers that were, like, two days old when she had it for dinner with my grandpa and my uncle. She would always go to this place a block away from her. Even when I would heat it, it would still taste disgusting. So yeah, my pizza trauma started at seven years old.

I remember when Giovanni invited me and his friends for pizza one time. This was back in the talking stage and I declined, not only because I hated pizza but because I am the biggest hater of his friends. Before going to bed, I texted him saying, "Hope you had a good time. Goodnight." He then replied, "That pizza was so disgusting, I regret going."

By the third day, he was already sitting with the popular kids. It wasn't because he was attractive but because of how rich he was. At first, I thought he gave off vibes that he was a stuck-up, snobbish rich boy, but then once I got to know him, I realized he put his money to good use and was very humble. For his first birthday at this school, he gave each student from the high school Jimmy Johns. He had us write our first and last names on a piece of paper and what we wanted to order. I was number forty-three on the list and I ordered something called the Turkey Tom.

He never told the popular kids he was rich. It was spread around by this girl named Jennifer who was obsessed with gossip. She searched him up and found out that his mother was a fashion designer with two children and that they were all from Venice, Italy.

He loved Italy and misses it there. He keeps telling me he is going to take me there one day, but I have no desire to go. I had never told him that, but I pretended to act excited about it. I was going to go, though, since he was going to pay for my plane ticket and buy me endless amounts of gelato. Maybe if I live off of gelato for the duration I'm there, Dad and my aunties will get off my back on how I never eat.

Once the popular kids found out he was worth hella money, they then decided to bring him to their friend group. He realized a few months later that they only liked him because of the wealth status and clout he got from his mother, so he found another group of friends.

I never liked his mother. She was xenophobic, frequently towards Chinese people and Southeast Asians. She told me I was okay, though, because "the Koreans and Japanese were good." I didn't like what she would say about other groups of people, so I recorded her. One day, I will be exposing her when I break up with Giovanni.

Giovanni even told me that, back in Italy, Damiano liked this girl who happened to be Chinese. She was born in Italy while her parents were from Shanghai, working in international business.

Their mother forced Damiano to stop seeing her or told him he would be on the streets of Venice. She was that brutal. Though she wouldn't let him see her anymore, he still follows her on Instagram and now she is in a relationship with someone else. I honestly think Ms. Laterza is that bitter because her man left her for an Asian woman.

Giovanni did mention one time that his father was no longer in their lives because he ended up hating how negative his mother was, and asked his children if they wanted to come with him or stay with their mother. For a reason I'm not sure of, the two boys chose their mother over him. He then left, being able to go wherever he wanted for business, and decided to live in Thailand because he loved the scenery. He's still there. He lives off of dragon fruit martinis, coconuts, and fish. Easy lifestyle, if you ask me.

Bitch-ass Giovanni had to miss the opportunity to live in a beach house and wake up in paradise every day, and instead chose to live with some miserable lonely woman. I wish his dumb-ass had taken the opportunity to live in Thailand because I would have never met him, then. In conclusion, if he had lived with his father, he would have been in Thailand the whole time, never having come to live in Ohio and living happily over there, instead.

According to Giovanni, his father has been married to his second wife for a while, maybe about seven years, and they have three children together—a boy and two girls. I've seen a photo of their family. They look about the same age and the dad looks very short.

His father contacts Giovanni and Damiano when he gets the chance, so maybe, like, twice a month, asking if they are planning to visit or maybe even considering living with him. Damiano has considered doing it, maybe, one day, but Giovanni doesn't want anything to do with him. Even when he talks to him through Facebook video call, he seems so out of it and just wants to hang up. His father still wants to talk to him twice a month. He does not get the hint.

I checked my Snapchat, which now has a feature called "random," and it brings up the time from March 17th when I recorded myself crying in the bathroom stall. It took me a minute to wonder why I was crying. I knew it had to be because of Satan-spawn, rat-burning, trifling, cupcake-eating-addicted Giovanni.

Then I remembered it was because of how he humiliated me in front of the whole school.

Right before he liked me, he had a crush on a girl named Malia, and admitted to me one time that he wanted to date her if homecoming night went well. Unfortunately for him, he didn't even get to go to homecoming with her. A week before, he had made a poster and asked her to homecoming along with giving her a bouquet of roses. She rejected him in front of everyone. I just want her to know, she dodged a motherfucking bullet.

I was crying because Giovanni exposed, in front of everyone, that I had hooked up with Junfeng. He was an exchange student from Fuzhou, China. This had happened two months before

Afterward, I had started dating Giovanni. I was hoping he would never find out about Junfeng, and when he went back to China, I thought I was safe from Giovanni finding out. But I wasn't, because Junfeng's stupid friends were talking about it in the boys' bathroom and Giovanni overheard.

"Have you fucked all of the men in Ohio or something? Because I know you fucked every man in this school!" he screamed so the whole cafeteria could hear.

"Stop . . ." I said calmly.

"How many men have you slept with? Be honest!" he shouted.

"I don't want to talk about this now."

"I'm not leaving until you tell me!"

"Okay—four, including you."

"Ugh, I've only slept with three girls including you, so now I feel weird that my girlfriend has slept with more people than me!"

His friend Travis then pulled him away and told him to get his act together. Once they had left, I stood there while everyone looked at me. I ran to the bathroom before anyone could see me burst into tears.

That was the most humiliating thing I've ever gone through in my life. I wanted to keep my sex life private, and now everyone in the whole cafeteria knew. At the time, I was anxious about what they thought of me. Did they think of me as dirty? A disgusting girl? Or even, easy? I don't know, and, looking back, they can think what they want. I know myself and I don't need to explain anything. I know that I am being cautious and that I am being responsible, so it is no one else's business.

I remember Giovanni told me he had lost his virginity to his ex-girlfriend back in Italy. Her name was Caterina and they were fourteen years old when they lost it to each other. She was pretty. She had long blonde hair and dark eyes. She also dressed very elegantly. They broke up a week before Giovanni left to live in the United States. She didn't take it well. She screamed and cried, wanting to make long-distance work, but Giovanni didn't want that.

The second girl he had sex with was a girl in our school named Aria. They hooked up on Giovanni's first day at school. She was a virgin prior, so she bled when they did it for the first time. He honestly did not know why that had happened and felt bad for her, but she said she was fine. They did it three more times and he said it was really enjoyable. He even said, "Why can't you do this like Aria?" before we were about to have sex one time. I was pissed. I left his house and we didn't talk for three days. He never apologized, either.

Right before that happened, Malik asked to hang out with me and a few other friends. I declined the offer because I wanted to respect the relationship I had with Giovanni. "Well, we can hang out as friends, of course, and I'd invite Makena and Braxton. Besides, doesn't he know I'm talking to Santana now?" Malik asked.

Makena and Malik are cousins, and the last time we all hung out we had a fun time at a bonfire. Braxton was his childhood friend from Cleveland who would visit Columbus once in a while.

During the three-day break I had from Giovanni, I responded to Malik and said that we should go ice skating and invite a few more people.

Makena came into the bathroom five minutes after me. She told me everything was going to be okay because she called him out in front of everyone, roasting him about being insecure and saying that he was nothing but a cupcake rat (inside joke) that everyone found funny.

I didn't talk to Giovanni the rest of the day, and I even avoided him the next day. Later that night, I heard the doorbell ring and opened the door to nothing but pink roses with a note peeking out saying, "I'm sorry." I ended up cutting the roses up and sending him a photo of them.

He realized that he wasn't forgiven just yet, so the following weekend he took me to the Melting Pot.

"So, am I forgiven?" he asked while holding the menu.

"You're lucky you're 6' 4"," I responded in a monotone voice while paying attention to the menu.

Speaking of height, I only date guys 6' 2" and above. My parents and I are 5' 7", but sometimes people think that my mom is taller because of my dad's stocky build. With me being that height, I need someone tall because I don't want to be taller than a man when I'm wearing heels, and I wear heels that can get pretty high. One time, Travis asked me out before I even knew Giovanni and I took a look at his height and politely declined. He was only 5' 10" so I had to pass. His wolf tattoo also gave me the ick.

His friend group was Natalie, Justin, Jacob, and Travis. I hate them all. Justin and Jacob are like the same person. They laugh in unison, they dress the same, and they always get haircuts together. Yes, they get the same style. It's creepy. The reason I don't like them is because they annoy everyone for fun and disrespect people's boundaries.

Travis is just rude for no reason. For example, he made a comment that everyone at my VS PINK-themed birthday party looked "cutesy" but that Amalia ruined the photos because of the "scary look" she had going on. He saw the posts of my birthday party because she posted them on her Instagram. Once Giovanni asked to see, he then turned to me and asked why he wasn't invited. Gio and I don't follow anyone we dislike. Natalie only follows friends, family, celebrities, and, for some reason, me. I will never follow that bitch back. Travis will follow anyone he knows, even if he doesn't like them. He always talks shit about people's posts that show up on his feed.

After Travis showed the pictures to Giovanni, I had to explain to him that it was a surprise birthday party my mom threw, and since she had heard us arguing three days before, she changed the birthday party to be girls only. It was Amina, Keira, Amalie, Makena, and my two neighbors, Kennedy and Anna.

She uninvited him because she believed it would cause me less stress for my birthday, which it did. He then yelled at me in front of everyone, which even made a teacher come out of her classroom. When that happened, Travis left the drama he had caused.

There would be instances where he would yell at me in public, a lot of times during school, and everyone would just stare. The only people who would step in were the teachers. The English teacher for the freshman classes even came out of her classroom one time and said, "Giovanni, what's wrong with you? Get your ass to class, right now."

Then there is Natalie, and words cannot describe how much I hate her "pick me" ass. She started calling me Hello Kitty as a racist joke, so the rest of his friend group started saying it too.

As macho as Giovanni was, he didn't defend me, so I defended myself.

"Hello Kitty is from Japan. I'm Korean, you stupid Bugs Bunny –looking ass bitch," I yelled at her.

"Why are you so mean to my friends?" He then started defending them. Typical.

"The real world is harsh, Gio. This is only an appetizer," I responded.

"Ouch," whispered Natalie.

"Ohhh, don't worry. You might be stupid, but something you have going for you is your big tits. It will get you pretty far."

"Apologize right now!"

"Or what? Are you going to hit me? Again?" I then walked away.

No girls at our school like Natalie anymore. In early high school, she had this group of friends who were girls but they all kicked her out of the group the day after homecoming because she humiliated them in front of their dates. Good for those girls for putting their foot down. About time.

It wasn't the first time she had done that. The girls let it go on for a while and then they realized they had had enough that night. There was another incident that happened before that, though, and I'm surprised that wasn't their last straw. It was when I, Giovanni, Natalie, and her former friend, Anna, snuck into a 21+ bar (their idea, not mine) but I decided to go because I was pissed at my parents that night, and needed a few shots.

While Giovanni was in the bathroom, I stayed with Natalie and then noticed that Anna was gone. We were stupid. Giovanni and I split off from them to do our own thing at the bar at some point during the night, and I regret that.

I asked Natalie where Anna had gone, and she smiled and said, "Oh, she went home with some cute guy." I responded with, "You're a piece of shit for letting her go to some random guy's place. Why is my boyfriend friends with dumbasses like you?"

Once I said that, her smile went away quickly and she started crying. As she was heading to the bathroom to cry, Giovanni came out to where I could see him, saying, "What's wrong?" Natalie shook her head and then ran into the bathroom. He came towards me and asked what had happened, so I told him not to worry about it.

He shrugged his shoulders and started dancing with a random crowd.

I then found Anna's location on Snapchat, and found a small house that was fifteen minutes away. I pick-pocketed Giovanni's keys. Although on average it would have been a fifteen-minute drive, I made it there in ten minutes.

The door to get inside was open, but the door to go inside the room they were in was locked. I got a coin from the kitchen counter and opened it. The man inside held us at gunpoint but the police came about a minute later.

Giovanni and Natalie had needed to get an Uber home. The following morning, he came over to my house and didn't say anything. We went up to my room and I tried to hug him. He then pushed me away and slapped me across the face. He threw my coat onto my bed, as I had left it at the bar the night before. He stomped out of my room and walked himself out the front door.

I'm friends with one of the girls in Natalie's former friend group. Her name is Courtney and she would talk about how Natalie would borrow their clothes without returning them. The only piece of apparel she did suggest returning was a pair of underwear, but Courtney said she could keep them, especially since during that time there was a rumor that she had an STD.

I remember when the rumor spread. Some girl's boyfriend spread it around the whole school, saying she got it from someone from another school. The rumor died down for a while, until a couple of years later, when they found a pair of red panties in the hallway with hella discharge in it. Some disgusting football player picked it up in front of his friends and said, "Hey, maybe it's Natalie's!" and laughed. When he said that, other people in the hallway heard it, and then the rumor started spreading again.

She was ugly-crying in the bathroom for a whole class period. I only know because Amalie and I walked in on her and I almost felt bad, until I remembered that time when Giovanni embarrassed me in the cafeteria, she was laughing, too, so we didn't comfort her at all. "Natalie's pretty upset right now. Can you comfort her?" Giovanni texted right after I left the bathroom.

"No, the fuck." I responded and went to English class.

What's crazy is that Natalie had a situationship who ghosted her when the scandal of her having an STD spread to his school a week later. Giovanni told me about it and asked me to comfort her once again, but I said no again. He wants me to get along so badly with her because they are besties.

Two weeks later, I found out that her situationship was my first friend when I came to America, as he was my dad's friend's son. We used to play tag with other kids from his neighborhood a lot. We stopped hanging out that much but would talk when his dad invited us to parties the family had. The party his dad invited us to was his and his wife's 20th wedding anniversary, and we talked about what had been going on in our lives. He told me that he ghosted a girl from my school because she had an STD. I asked, "Was her name Natalie?" and his eyes widened from shock and he said, "YEAHHH. YOU KNOW HER?"

I was like, "Yes, she's best friends with Giovanni." I was aware she didn't have an STD but I didn't want him to go back to her, so I didn't say anything. It's already bad that I have to see her hanging out with my boyfriend, but her hanging out with my other friends? I will not let it happen!

I realized I've made her cry a lot. It's not good for my character, but whatever. I needed the last laugh. I once noticed that Natalie was wearing baggy clothes for one day, so I asked her, "Are you pregnant?!" and she freaked out and responded so fast with a no. Then she ran to the bathroom and cried.

"Why would you ask her that?!" Giovanni turned to me.

"I thought it was funny." I laughed.

"So mean, dude," Travis responded.

A part of me felt threatened by her as well. I remember when I went to his house one day, I was curious who he had on Snapchat. So while he was showering, I opened his phone and scrolled through the list. I was displeased when I clicked on Natalie's name and found a text message from when we were three weeks into dating that said, "Never bring up that kiss again. It was one time and I don't like you like that." Then after that, he kept begging her to unsave what she said, but she said, "No! Good luck!" with a smiley emoji. I didn't want him to know that I knew, but I still wanted to bring it up because maybe if I talked about how it bothered me, he would respect my boundaries and they would stop talking.

"Have you and Natalie ever done anything?" I asked.

"Like what?"

"I don't know. Her give you a blow job, kiss, hold hands?" I lean in closer.

"Trust me, it was in the past. She seriously means nothing to me but I like her as my friend." It took a few seconds for him to respond.

I was straightforward with him that I wasn't comfortable with that and that it always bothers me whenever I see her, but they are still friends to this day. Ugh, I can't stand her. Every time I think of her, I start to feel like a plankton when he's angry, like turning red, forehead veins popping out and shit.

While I hated Giovanni's friend group, he hated mine. My friends in high school were Makena, Amalie, and Keira. He didn't like Makena because she would always call out his behavior when I told her our problems. He didn't like Amalie because she was considered too much of a feminist for him, which annoyed the shit out of him. He didn't like Keira because she didn't acknowledge his presence, and I was on Keira's side on that one. I wanted him to know that none of us liked his attitude and that if you want respect from someone, then you need to earn it.

Giovanni respected the cultures I had ties to, which was the bare minimum. I just wish he would defend me when someone would make fun of my background. I didn't care if it was someone on the street, or someone he didn't like, or his friends or his family—I expected him to call anyone out that would disrespect me.

One time I told Makena about the comments Natalie would make, about calling me Hello Kitty.

I told Makena not to say anything to them but she didn't listen.

So one day at school she called Gio out about it when talking to his friends at the locker. "Hey, what is this shit I hear about you not defending my best friend?"

"Huh?" he responded.

"This bitch is making fun of her and you're not even defending your girlfriend? Rather siding with Miss Girl who looks like she enjoys the presence of Bugs Bunny? Like, are you into this 'pick me' bitch?"

After hearing that, Natalie cried and ran to the bathroom. I was there and I giggled a little bit. Giovanni then looked at me with a death stare so I controlled myself and stopped. C'mon, it was funny, and maybe if she wasn't racist she wouldn't be made fun of. Like, I'm so against bullying, but bullying racists? Now that's another story.

I promise, Makena is really sweet and the most supportive person ever. She acts like that if she feels provoked, and Natalie would provoke her a few times, causing Makena to lash out at her like that.

Makena can relate to similar comments I've gotten because we do share one of the same ethnic groups and it is a predominately white school, so, honestly, these stupid comments are going to happen. I didn't know Makena was Korean until a few months after becoming friends. She had kimchi for lunch one day so I asked, "Oh wow, you like kimchi too?" and she responded, "My mom makes the best kimchi ever. She used to work in a restaurant back in Seoul."

Makena is Black from her father's side and Korean from her mother. Her mother was born in the capital, which is Seoul, and moved to Ohio to be able to live with her dad. Our moms are close friends, although my mom doesn't like talking about Korea as much, and I never understood why until she told me this morning. They do speak in Korean and talk about Korean culture frequently, but anything about the country of South Korea, mom tends to avoid. She ends up changing the subject quickly.

Makena, these twins two grades younger than us, and a boy who is a grade younger than us were the only Asians at this school. However, with how the demographics work, Makena and I wouldn't be counted under Asian—we would be under "two or more races."

The twins were from Chiang Mai, Thailand, and moved here when they were seven. Rodney played soccer and basketball while Ashton liked hiking and drawing. I only know this because Mom is friends with their mom.

Their parents own a small Thai restaurant down the street from us, so we would always go out and eat at their place. Each time I would order the Bangkok chicken wings.

During my freshman year, there was an exchange student from the Philippines named Jade. She had short black hair with bangs and purple braces. She was about 5' 4". She came to the United States and stayed with Jenna Bianchi's family. She came because she got into a fight with her mom, so her mom decided to send her away for a while. Jade was a very quiet girl and didn't have that many friends at school, but once you got to know her, she would tell the funniest stories and make you cry laughing. I was sad when she left. The last thing she said to me was, "I hope you visit me in the Philippines one day," and gave me a man in a barrel. I didn't realize the barrel could be taken out until I put it on my desk. I was in for a surprise.

I was looked at as racially ambiguous. With my golden-brown skin tone, almond-shaped eyes, straight black hair, and thick eyebrows, I'd get numerous guesses on what my cultural background was.

I've gotten Peruvian, Indigenous American, Ecuadorian, or Polynesian in the past. I then would say, "Well, I'm Korean a—" and they would be like, "Really? No wayyyy."

Americans are so obsessed with race, and it might not be an annoying question to everyone but it was to me. So I stopped answering, because everyone I met had that same first question. I would then start saying, "I don't know," and walk away. People would guess my background was like a never-ending game that I never asked to play.

Amalie was the only white girl in our friend group. She's never said anything sus but I feel sus about her parents. With how her mother's casserole looked, I just knew something was off.

Amalie was this goth girl into heavy metal and the way she dressed would intimidate others, even though she is super sweet. She has piercings all over her face that her mom disapproves of, but Amalie couldn't give a shit. A lot of times, when her parents would piss her off, she would get another tattoo somewhere on her body. She even spent some of the money her parents saved for her for college to get some of those tattoos.

"Are you proud of what you did?" Amalie's mom barged into her room while I was on FaceTime with her.

"What are you talking about Mom?" she responded rudely.

"I know you spent part of the college money your father gave you to get some tattoos, Amalia!"

"Oh, shit . . ."

I felt awkward witnessing that so I quickly hung up and finished the partner assignment we were supposed to be doing on Facetime by myself, and sent her a picture of my answers.

Amalie has no idea if she even wants to go to college. For a while now, she has been stuck on what she wants to do in the future. Her parents are forcing her to go to college and she will go, but if she doesn't like it during the first month, then she's dropping out. She left out that part when talking to her parents.

Makena is going to Kent State to pursue a career in fashion and Keira is going to the University of Cincinnati to major in nursing. I never would have thought that Keira was going to go into that program. She hated science courses, especially chemistry. If she switches majors by the second year, I wouldn't be surprised. I can see her being in an art-related major, like animation, and I suggested it to her a few times. But she cares about making her parents proud and following her mother's footsteps, since she is also a nurse.

4

Giovanni is currently attending the University of Cincinnati. He comes home every two weekends. He applied to Ohio State University, Miami University, the University of Cincinnati, and Ohio University. He had a 4.0 GPA and got into all schools.

I applied to Miami University, the University of Cincinnati, Bowling Green State University, Kent State University, Michigan State University, and Ohio State University. I graduated high school with a 3.7, getting into all schools except for Ohio State.

I was embarrassed that I didn't get in so I took the letter and burned it in the fireplace when no one was home. Mom asked what happened to going to Ohio State so I lied, saying I never ended up applying. I'm taking this secret to my grave.

Giovanni was expecting me to go to UC with him, but right after I toured Bowling Green, I immediately changed my mind. I promised Giovanni that I would go to UC, but it's not like I pinky promised.

When I told Giovanni that I was going to BGSU we got into a heated argument. I was sitting on his bed and he was moving things on his desk while we were discussing it. He then grabbed his football helmet and threw it towards me, hitting my neck. He claimed it was an accident.

His mom came in asking if everything was alright. I said yes and then left. I drove home crying, blasting the song "Good for You" by Olivia Rodrigo. I wasn't crying from the physical pain but the treatment he gave me almost every day.

With all the boys my friends and I have in our life, we need fucking therapy. Giovanni punches holes in the walls, Amalie's ex got her pregnant and then abandoned her, and Makena's situationship wanted to date her and then marry her in three months. As you can tell, we've dealt with some crazy bastards.

Amalie had the worst out of all of us, for real. When Amalie found out the news that she was pregnant, she was terrified of telling her parents and her boyfriend at the time. Her parents were disappointed but, since they were pro-life, they wanted her to continue the pregnancy and have the kid. She was excited to have a kid. A lot of times she would talk about having a mini-me, and she finally had the opportunity.

She called her boyfriend, feeling bubbly, but all he said was, "Oh . . ." and then hung up the phone. He then immediately ghosted her. He went to another school and wouldn't open the door when Amalie came over to his house. She eventually gave up on him but she never gave up on the unborn child. Due to the immense amount of stress, she ended up miscarrying.

She cried so hard into my arms a lot of times and there would be times I would even cry with her. She never deserved that and I hope that she will find the right person to have a family with when she is ready.

I definitely think that my situation could have been easily avoided if I wasn't stupid enough to stay. I just loved him so much I felt like I couldn't leave. I feel like college is the only choice I have to start fresh in my life.

The reasons I chose Bowling Green were because I loved the atmosphere, I got the most scholarships from them, and going there gave me every chance to get the hell away from Gio. I don't regret my decision because I need to prioritize myself first. He would also tutor me and other students in math because he was an A+ student in the course. But when he dealt with me, I would always end up crying, right after he screamed and threw the book across the room out of frustration. Making someone cry after yelling at them for not understanding the homework was a dad's job, not a boyfriend's.

I'm excited to start college in August. I will be majoring in accounting. During my junior year of high school, I went on a tour with Mom and Amina. I honestly didn't think it was going to be so much fun. We played ping-pong with some students and got a free meal.

Right before we left, they gave us a tote bag to put our freebies in. We got a tumbler with the BGSU mascot, a sweatshirt, and a T-shirt that had the name of the school on it.

I was stuck between attending Ohio State or BGSU, but I found out very early in my senior year that I was rejected from Ohio State. I wasn't bummed about it because I had already gotten into other schools that I could work with.

Right when I started senior year, before I found out my status, I toured Ohio State with Giovanni. I told him I wanted to tour colleges for freebies and picture-taking when, in reality, I was looking at schools that I wanted to go to. I regret taking him with me because he complained about all the walking we had to do, and then he fucking decided to fake being sick so we could end the tour early. I guess it's okay, though, because I ended up getting free stuff: a T-shirt, a Buckeyes milk-chocolate box, and pens.

5

Nari and I have a close relationship although she can be annoying at times. If I don't have plans with friends or Giovanni, then I'm more than likely with her. She is very quiet outside of the house but when she is home she talks so much that Mom tells her to shut up.

Nari never really liked Giovanni. The first time she met him he said hi and she just waved and stared while holding her pumpkin-spotted Build-a-Bear cat she brings everywhere. She's had it since she was five.

"I feel a weird presence with him. . . ." she said after he went out the front door.

"What do you mean?" I asked.

"There's something off about him, and it's not because he smells like AXE deodorant."

I didn't listen to my little sister and I wish I would have. He started to get controlling a week later. I thought it was punishment for my past that he wasn't fond of. When I got out of the car that night, he grabbed my wrist tightly and didn't let me go until I kissed him back.

When he got home, he texted me back but I didn't text him back for two days, so he knew he had to make it up to me. On the third day, he came to my front door and delivered a giant llama plush from FYE. I felt guilty for not forgiving him so I accepted his apology.

A lot of times he bought me a plushie because he knew I would forgive him easily. When we were in the talking stage, I would show him cute stuffed animals but I told him I shouldn't be wasting my money on that stuff, so he remembered what I had said and decided to buy them for me.

He gave me a turtle when he bruised my knee, a pink frog from Build-a-Bear when he grabbed me by the hair, and a Baphomet squishable plush on my birthday. My favorite was the Baphomet plush, not because it was from a good memory we had together but because it was the cutest one he got me.

I attempted to leave the relationship a year in, but then he started to change his ways and even stopped hitting me. That only lasted for a month. No matter how much he changes or what type of gifts he gives me, nothing will make up for the trauma he has caused.

6

Dad keeps calling me down for breakfast. Today we are eating a little later than usual, as we are done with school for now and have been getting up a bit later. Before I go downstairs, I hide my Jack Daniels and tequila bottles by covering them with a cardigan and putting them deep into my walk-in closet.

"Didn't know we were eating like Americans today," I say as Dad puts the sausage and pancakes on my plate.

"Oh, so moody today. Cheer up, my princess." He pinches my cheek.

I lose my appetite. If I eat anything, I feel like I'm going to throw up afterward. I can't eat, but if Dad sees that I'm not eating then he's going to find out why. I'm able to get a few bites of the sausage in but I really can't eat any more of it.

"What is wrong with you lately? You are usually so energetic," asks Dad.

"Well, Vangelis, I wanted to talk to you about this later today but the sooner the better . . ." Mom jumped in.

"You can always talk to me." Dad put his hand on my bruised shoulder.

"Ow! No, it's okay Vati."

"Remember that guy she is going out with? Yeah, well, he's a hitter!" blurts Nari.

"Nari! I swear to god, I'm going to take your pumpkin-spotted cat and rip its head off!" I scream and get up from the table.

"Athena, calm down. Nari, go to your room, honey," Mom says as she holds me back.

Nari stuffs the chocolate chip pancakes Dad made this morning in her mouth and runs straight to her room. As I am being held back by Mom and Dad, I start bawling my eyes out.

"Athena, calm down and show me your arms," Dad says calmly.

"Once you let me go."

I hesitate but eventually I take off my fuzzy jacket, revealing a scratch near my elbow and a bruise on my wrist and right shoulder. Dad is petrified.

"I've noticed you will even wear jackets and pants during the summer and I've never understood why. Now I do," he says, rubbing his forehead due to stress.

"I'm sorry, Vati . . ."

"You don't owe me an apology. You just need to answer questions for me." Dad sits on the couch with mom rubbing his back.

"Okay . . ." I say quietly, sitting on the living room floor.

"So, Giovanni . . . he did this to you?"

"Yes . . ."

"Did he get his US citizenship yet?" he asks, randomly.

"Not yet. Why?"

"Tell him to say goodbye to the American dream," he says as he walks to his office.

I have no idea what he is up to, but I am scared. I cry even harder once he leaves, so mom has me go to the couch and covers me with our Korean mink-fleece red blanket.

"Athena, babe, I promise: when you break up with him, everything will get better." She grabs a tissue and starts wiping my tears away.

"I don't know. I've been meaning to do this, but I'm scared, Mom."

"I know it's hard, but just know, if you need me, I will be right there. Even if you wanted me right there in the room with you guys, I would be there."

"Thank you, Mama."

I know I'm going to be traumatized by Giovanni for a long time, I don't even know if the painful memories of him will go away. Nari suggested therapy but mom is against it; she thinks it's a scam. I honestly want to try at least three sessions, and if it doesn't work out for me, then I won't do it anymore.

Last week I told my mom that I had problems. I kept it vague and told her that "there is stuff going on in my life and I would like to try and see a therapist."

"Athena, therapy is a scam. You know you can talk to me," she said calmly.

"But I don't think you can help me," I said.

"That's not nice!"

"Well, what's not nice is that you took Nari and I to this shitty country and had our lives change completely! Now that's not fucking nice," I screeched.

"Okay, fine. We will try therapy. Give me my phone and don't ever talk to me like that again," she said as I turned around and walked away, tears filling my eyes.

I hated America. I hated living here. I never had a traumatizing memory back in Munich, but at least every week here, I witness something disturbing. I remember when I was fifteen, I started experimenting with drugs. I did shrooms once. I had so many hallucinations that it scared me. Once I stopped hallucinating, I grabbed my diary and wrote down everything I saw and everything I heard. I hid the diary in my closet, but then I forgot that I had done that. The next week, when Mom was doing spring cleaning, she found it. I was in the living room watching the Bratz movie. She came up to me, smacked the popcorn bucket out of my hands, grabbed me by the wrist, and took me to my room. She grabbed the yellow lighter on my particle-board desk and burned the diary in front of me. She also found my 750ml bottle of Malibu strawberry rum hiding under my cardigan in the closet, so she took that, opened the window, and threw it out the window, making the bottle break. It was a cold winter day, about 25 degrees, and she made me go outside and pick everything up if I didn't want her telling Vati.

7

Taking two minutes to list as many reasons as I can think of on why I love Giovanni:

• We go on fun dates

Besides that one Aria comment, he makes me feel like I'm the only girl in the world. He doesn't compliment other girls and he doesn't say other girls are attractive. At least, not in front of me.

He's the one who gives me the most attention. Other guys would play video games for hours while their girlfriends wait for them, only finishing when it was time to go to bed. He isn't a gamer anyway. He would respond to my messages as soon as possible, even when he was out with his friends.

• He made sure I always felt beautiful

• He would write me cute love letters

• He made sure to learn about my interests. I always appreciated art, so we would go on art-museum dates and we would do paint DIYs that I found on TikTok or Pinterest

• Never made me feel insecure about my looks; instead, he would tell me how much he loved my features

Once I fell in love with him, that's when he started hitting me. I guess if he knew that I was in love with him, then it would be almost impossible for me to leave.

I took a sociology class and we were on the topic of domestic violence for a week. Mrs. Anatova started off the topic with a warning: If it's too triggering for you, you can step out and there will be an alternative assignment. I wanted to step out so bad but I thought that if I did, it was going to be obvious. One student did step out and did the other assignment. He didn't go through it himself, but he witnessed his mother going through it by her ex-boyfriend. While she was hospitalized, he stayed with his aunt for two weeks. He said it was the most traumatic experience of his life as his mother almost died.

On the third day we were talking about domestic violence in the class, we watched a documentary on the child's perspective, It basically showed what the child witnessed when a parent was a victim of domestic violence. Right when the dad slapped the mom on the face, I got triggered. I had a rapid heartbeat and I felt like I couldn't breathe. I couldn't watch the rest of the video, so I left the classroom. I think I was triggered because Gio and I had talked about having kids once. He said that our little girl would probably have dark brown hair and amber-colored eyes, with an olive skin tone. The daughter in the video resembled what Giovanni described.

When I got home from school that day, I took a lot of time to think about our relationship. It made me realize that if we did have a kid, the kid would more than likely be abused by him too.

One time, he got into an argument with his mother at the kitchen table. As it got worse, he ended up pushing her. He then realized who he did that to and started backing away. His mother then threw water in his face and then threw the glass on the floor and left the kitchen. The maid ended up cleaning it up.

* * *

On our first anniversary, Gio surprised me with tickets to go to Otherworld. It was an immersive art museum that I had been dying to go to ever since it opened. One of the last exhibits we entered was this place that had a couch along with a vintage record player that controlled chill music. We found a CD that had the closest vibe to a romantic setting. I was sitting on top of him with my legs on the couch making out. We were so into it that we didn't even notice that a man and his two toddlers had entered the exhibit until the man cleared his throat. We then walked away in shame, like Adam and Eve when they were forced to leave the Garden of Eden.

Even though what Giovanni did to me was wrong, I thought I had to be grateful that he only had eyes for me. That's only the bare minimum, and my eighteen-year-old self sees it now. At the time, I was grateful for him never calling another woman pretty, hot, or sexy, I had to be grateful that he never followed Instagram models, or liked a girl's bikini picture. He even told me that he didn't watch porn because it would be considered cheating in a relationship.

I consider it cheating, too, and no matter what, you will always find out if your partner is cheating sooner or later. So if he is watching it behind my back, I will find out somehow.

The last good memory I had with Giovanni was about two weeks ago. We watched *The Hunger Games*, my favorite movie. I remember when the movie first came out, I joined so many fandoms. I even made internet friends from it. There was Alice from England and Adelina from New Jersey. I don't talk to Alice anymore but Adelina I talk to from time to time. I still have both of them on Instagram. Alice was the same age as me and Adelina is two years older than me. She is currently engaged and she has been with the girl for about three years.

I like the whole *Hunger Games* series but nothing tops the first one. My favorite character was Clove. Her sadistic tendencies spoke to me—I don't know how to explain it. Something I wish they had included were the scenes of the mutts being actual fallen tributes. In the book, Katniss describes Glimmer's mutation as having blonde fur and emerald-colored eyes, with a collar that says 1. In the movie, the mutts have no distinct feature that implies they were fallen tributes.

I watched *The Hunger Games* two days after it came out. I went with my friend, her mom, and her older sister. Dad didn't want me to watch it because he checked the parent's guide and had seen that there would be a lot of gore, but I still went anyway. I told him that I was going to watch *The Lorax*. I hate *The Lorax*. I always had beef with the character because of my pure hatred for the color orange. Ever since I started picking out my own clothes, I have never owned anything orange, nor have even had a piece of clothing that had orange in it.

I also thought Cato was so cute. He reminded me of my first crush, although they looked nothing alike. The only reason he reminded me of my fifth-grade crush, Jasper, was because of the blonde hair with the same haircut and green eyes. My friends thought we would have been cute and always urged me to talk to him, but I never had the confidence. He moved away the summer we finished sixth grade and I have no idea what happened to him.

Update: I tried to see if Jasper had an Instagram but nothing showed up. I found his Facebook, though. His profile picture was him with his family. It took me a second to find him; he looks unrecognizable. His hair grew longer, he lost a lot of weight, and now he has a beard. I knew it was him when I saw his "about him" section. Born in Columbus, Ohio, lives in Toledo, Ohio, and will be attending Cleveland State University in the fall. In his likes and interests, there was *Total Drama Island.* He used to talk about it all the time in class with his friends.

His favorite character was Harold, but I hated Harold with a passion. Leshawna was cool, though. My favorite character had to be Gwen. It was like I had to *be* her, and I was, for Halloween when I was twelve. Looking back, those photos are super embarrassing and my mom won't take them down from her Facebook page. There's something with her and "cherishing memories forever."

This upcoming fall, I'm planning to visit Miami University again, where Amina will dress up as Dr. Doofenshmirtz while I'm going to be Perry the Platypus.

8

This is my last date I'm having with Giovanni and he has no fucking idea. He's taking me out to a steakhouse tonight. I'm going to wear my emerald-green backless mini-dress he got me from Windsor two weeks ago.

I'm going to be careful with my words tonight. I'm not going to be the sassy girl that ends up getting me in trouble in the end and it's because I am craving a juicy, buttered-up lobster.

Right when we enter the restaurant, I feel weird stares from everyone. I look down to make sure I don't have a nip slip, and I don't. I made sure my red lipstick wasn't smudged. It wasn't, so what could it be?

"Gio, why are we getting scolded by these old dudes?" I whisper.

"Because if you looked at the prices then you would know that they probably think we are some immature teens who might dine and dash," he laughed.

Giovanni never flexed his money to strangers in the way that other people with clout might. He let people have all those assumptions about him because, in a way, he was more at peace. Even though he kept his wealth private from others, he did brag about it to me a few times and, I won't lie, it kind of annoyed me.

Giovanni's house has nine bedrooms with walk-in closets and bathrooms in each room. He is super spoiled by his mom. He relies on her money until after he graduates college. He's never worked a day in his life, while I have a job that I work at in the summer. Which reminds me, I start very soon, in like, two weeks. I'll stop complaining when I get to sit on my ass all day, like he does.

I work at Rue 21, a retail store at my local mall. A lot of the clothes are cute, while others can be questionable, due to some having stupid quotes or words on them. When I first started working there, I didn't even tell him. He found out himself because he needed to get a hold of me: apparently I was in trouble. He found out through my location that he made me share with him.

He would come to my work so often because I was in trouble a lot, and he would come just to talk to me about the issues we had. I wanted to resolve our issues when my shift ended, but that didn't work out for him—he always needed things resolved immediately. It got so bad that one of my managers got pissed off at both of us and she threatened to fire me, so I told Giovanni that if I got fired, I would dump him, so he eventually stopped.

Without looking at the prices, I order the steak, the lobster, and a fresh strawberry-mango cooler mocktail. I have barely eaten all day, and I hadn't even eaten yesterday from all the stress and anxiety. But today, I am able to manage eating everything on the plate, even the asparagus they serve with the steak, and I hate asparagus.

We leave the restaurant and he takes me home. As I am about to leave, he wants me to stay.

"Please don't leave Athena. I missed you."

"I missed you too, Gio," I respond quietly.

"No, I really, really missed you. I know it's been only a few days but I really can't imagine my life without you. You're all I have in this world and I'm grateful you're here with me," he says, while rubbing my hand gently with his thumb.

Fuck, he is guilt-tripping me now.

"Please stay with me tonight. I don't want to be alone," he says.

"Well, isn't Damiano home for the summer? Plus, your mom is there," I say.

"Yeah, but still, I don't feel love from them the way that you always give it to me. Just, please stay the night Athena. . . . We can do whatever you want."

"Anything?" I start considering sleeping over.

"Yes, anything, babe."

"Okay, well, I want to watch *The Princess and The Pauper*."

"From *Barbie*?" He rasies his left eyebrow.

"Do you want me to stay with you tonight or not?"

"Yes, okay, we'll watch it."

"Perfect." I grin.

Getting to do something I wanted makes me feel like I won until three seconds later, when I remember I am supposed to break up with him tonight. We make some buttery popcorn from his popcorn machine that is located in his living room. We then take the jumbo bucket and go into his room to watch the movie.

"You know, I had a great time with you today, baby girl," he says, while I internally cringe.

He doesn't call me that often but when he does, it makes me wanna vomit. What makes men think that that is a cute nickname? It gives me the ick. You know what else gives me the ick? Using emojis while having a deep conversation. Like, stop sending me the "100" emoji after the sentence "Meeting you was the best thing that ever happened to me."

"I had a great time today with you too." I honestly only had a great time because I ate good. He leans in to kiss me, but I reject the kiss.

"It's Preminger's song, it's a bop," I joke, while taking a handful of popcorn and shoving it into my mouth.

9

After Giovanni drops me off the next morning, I go to Makena's house to talk about my crisis. I ring the doorbell and she opens the door with Keira and Amalie sitting in the living room.

"You guys are all here?" I ask as I walk through the front door.

"Yeah, we tried getting a hold of you in the group chat and I private messaged you, too," says Makena.

"Oh, sorry, my phone must have been on Do Not Disturb," I respond.

I remember that I turned off my notifications for Snapchat because whenever I get a notification, Giovanni always wants to see the message and see what I'm doing. I'm not cheating on him or anything, but my friends are always talking shit about him, so that's what I have to worry about.

"I needed someone to talk to about something going on." I take a seat on the couch.

"You said yes to coming with my family to the Bahamas later in the summer?" Keira asks excitedly.

"No, I'm too broke for that."

"Well, what is it then?" Keira asks.

"Well, I've decided that I should leave Giovanni . . ." I say, starting to choke up.

"Thank god. You knew we never liked him anyway." Makena says.

Amalie is the only one to notice that I am going to start bawling my eyes out, so she comes right to me and hugs me tightly.

"Makena, Keira, Amalie. There's something I've been keeping from you guys that I didn't want to talk about . . ."

"Okay, what's going on? You know you can tell us anything," says Amalie.

I take off my jacket, revealing the bruises, and they are all horrified. Makena even covers her mouth.

"Athena . . . how could you keep something like this from us?" asked Makena.

"I was scared, Makena." I cry even more.

"Please, break up with him right now. This isn't okay. I'm also calling the cops."

"No, please. I will take care of it."

"Clearly you won't, if it has already gotten this far. We are here for you and we are worried. Break up with him now." She hands me my phone.

Through Snapchat, I text him that I'm breaking up with him and then quickly turn off my phone. I take a deep breath and everyone starts staring at me.

"Are you okay, Athena?" Keira asks while Amalie comforts me by hugging me.

"I'm fine guys. I promise. Let's play some Monopoly. It will help me get things off my mind." Ten minutes into the game, Mom calls me, saying I need to be home right now. I swear if it's about the glass I forgot to wash, I will scream.

Before going on my date with Giovanni, I had drunk some grape juice and was going to wash the glass I had used when I got home after the date, but I ended up sleeping over. Mom hates dishes in the sink even if it's a spoon. If we use it, we are expected to wash it right after. "Mom, if it's about the glass I forgot to wash, I'm sorry. I didn't expect to spend the night at someon—" I say as she cuts me off.

"Forget about the glass. Look who is in the living room," she responds.

"You let him in?" I whisper.

I hurry home. My heart drops right as I take my first step in. It is Giovanni. I'm shaking. He gets closer and closer to me and I start hyperventilating.

"Hey . . . what's wrong?" he asks.

I'm confused, because why is he comforting me when I broke up with him less than half an hour ago? I'm expecting a slap in the face for doing that to him, but he is hugging me?

"Am I in trouble?" I question.

"No, I was expecting a text back because you haven't answered since you left my place. I wanted to know if you were home safe."

"Oh, yeah. I stopped by Makena's and then got home just now."

"Well, that's good to know you got home safe. I was worried." He then hugs me and leaves.

When I look back on Snapchat, I find out that the message was never even sent. Due to my state of panic, I forgot that her Wi-Fi connection could get shitty at times. That's why we mainly go to the library or my house to get our work done.

I tell her to tell her parents to fix it but she tells me they've been procrastinating about getting it fixed. It's been two years. Her parents are always busy working and are barely ever at the house until the evening time, when they eat dinner and spend time with the family. But Makena needs stable Wi-Fi for her school work.

10

I've been in my room since noon yesterday. It's already 8 a.m. I got a lot of sleep after drinking the rest of the Jack Daniels bottle. I now have a hangover, but it's . . . whatever. I took the Jack Daniels bottle from my dad's shelf of alcohol in the basement. He has SKYY Vodka, Patron Silver Tequila, Jack Daniels, Hennessy, and Blue Moon cans. He doesn't drink that much, only when there is a get-together at our house, but that seldom happens since COVID hit, so he won't notice the Hennessy missing. Once I'm old enough, I'll replace it for him, and even by that time I know he still won't find out.

Seeing my parents' relationship makes me kind of jealous when Giovanni gives me a bad day. My parents would argue here and there but my dad would never raise his voice at Mom, let alone have the urge to hit her, so Dad hearing that Giovanni beat my ass was something that made his blood boil.

There was one incident where my one aunt back in Germany was in a relationship with a man for maybe two months, until Dad made her leave the relationship. I remember being in the living room watching *The Aristocats* and I overheard them arguing.

"Well, how about you shut the fuck up, bitch?!" he yelled.

"Please don't yell at me! It hurts my feelings," she said, while crying and yelling.

He had been picking me up in the car and I told him exactly what I had heard when they were in the kitchen. It gave me an excuse to swear at six years old. After he heard what I'd said, he slammed on the brakes, and I was scared I would be in trouble for saying "fuck" and "bitch." But it was actually because he had decided to turn around and go back to my aunt's house.

He made me wait in the car. I remember him getting out so quickly and locking the door in case her boyfriend was going to try to go after me. I don't know what he did, but I remember the boyfriend storming out of her house and we never saw him again.

Sometimes I would walk in to find my parents cuddling with each other, and mom looked so safe in his arms. Made me almost tear up at how beautiful it was. Most of the time when I would cuddle with Giovanni, I would have fear in my body. When cuddling with your partner, you're supposed to feel safe, like no one will harm you, but I didn't feel that way.

11

I get out of bed and take pictures of every injury he has given me. I know that I'm done with him and I'm ready to expose him for what he has done. I only showed people the bruises on my arms and the scratch near my elbow. There are also scratches on my stomach and thighs, but I didn't want to show that part of my body to anyone.

Those scratches were from when he wanted me to keep listening to him about why it was wrong to ignore his text, but instead I had tried to leave the room. He grabbed me by the waist, wanting me to stay, but I kept urging him to let me go, and he ended up scratching me when I tried prying his hands off.

After showing Makena the pictures through Snapchat, she then saves the photos, which freaks me out. I beg her to unsave them but she won't unsave them until she arrives. She tells me she is on the way and I have no idea what to expect from her.

Makena knocks very loudly on the door and I run downstairs before Mom can reach the door.

While opening the door, I am out of breath. "Are you okay?" Makena asks, concerned.

"Yes. . . . Now let's go upstairs."

Silence arises while we are both walking up to my room. I close the door and drink half a bottle of water before Makena gets to the interrogation.

"Athena . . . I'm very concerned," she starts.

"I know, and I'm thankful you and our friends care about me, but I promise I will be fine. Just tell me what I can do to solve this on my own."

"The only way you can get help is to report this to the police. Athena, you can't do this on your own. It's okay to reach out for help."

"No, I can't do that."

"Yes, you can and you will."

"NO!" I start to cry and have a panic attack.

Makena opens the door and screams for Mom. She calls her again. I get so frustrated with her that I literally push her out of the room and lock my door.

Through the door, I can hear that Mom has come upstairs. "What's wrong?" Mom asks Makena.

"She's not coming out. . . . She showed me her body, full of scratches and bruises. She needs to report it."

"SHUT THE FUCK UP!" I scream.

"Athena, if you don't open this door right now, I'm getting your father to bust down this damn door."

"Go get him then!"

"Vangelis!" Mom screams at the top of her lungs.

"Dear, I'm cooking."

"Get your ass up here now! It's an emergency!"

Dad runs upstairs as fast as he can and I can feel him shaking the stairway area. "Athena, open this door please!" He twists the knob.

"NO!"

"If you don't open this door I'm coming in there one way or another."

"Go ahead!"

While I am bawling my eyes out, I can hear him trying to break through the door with the weight of his body. Knowing how strong he is, I go to the corner on the opposite side of my room and he manages to get in twenty seconds later. My door is broken horizontally, in half. This crazy bastard took down my door!

Makena and Mom come in after Dad and try to comfort me. I'm in the corner curled up, not wanting to be taken away from this area.

"Athena, we are only trying to help you. When you're with us, no one is going to hurt you," Mom says calmly.

"Okay. Just take my hand and we will solve this," Makena says.

"I can't . . ."

"Yes, you can. Athena, we need to go to the police department because this is very bad. Show them what you showed me."

"Listen to your friend," Mom says.

Makena drives us to the police station while Mom stays in the back with me. I have stopped crying but now I am using tissues to get out all the snot that has formed in my nose from sobbing my system out.

While sitting in the police office, I feel uneasy. I wasn't the one who did anything wrong. The policeman gives Makena and me a bottle of water. Mom is waiting outside of the office. I only wanted Makena with me so she respected the decision has stayed outside.

✳ ✳ ✳

Once I get home, I get into my comfy pajamas and lay in bed, covering myself up in my favorite cozy blue blanket from TJ Maxx. I honestly don't remember that much from the police office. Makena was there for moral support and did the talking for me. The only thing I did on my part was show the cops the pictures I had, but then they also asked to take photos themselves and keep them for evidence.

Makena and I talked for a few minutes and then she had to go home to take care of her younger brother while her parents went to work. She sat on the rocking chair and hesitated to say what she needed to say.

"I'm sorry Athena . . ." She says.

"For what?" I asked.

"For not reading you better," she said quietly with tears coming out of her eyes.

"What do you mean?"

"It's now starting to come to me. During last summer you would wear long-sleeved shirts and pants when it would be super hot outside. I felt like I should have noticed."

"No, I promise, you're not at fault here," I say while getting her a tissue.

Makena and I hold hands. I wanted to reassure her that everything was going to be okay. This has been the most stressful time of my life, but the fact that Makena, Amalie, Keira, Amalie, Mom, Dad, and even Nari, despite how young she is, have all been there for me—I don't even know how to thank them for the support.

Next Tuesday, I start therapy. My therapist is a woman named Leah Chen. I tried to find her on social media to see what she looked like and who she was. Instagram gave me no luck. I must have looked through twelve Leah Chens and I got nowhere. The first one was a college student, the second one was a girl who looked eleven years old, and the rest of them were just inactive accounts. I'm thinking that she has an inactive Instagram account.

The next place I checked was Facebook. I had more luck there. I set the filter to find a Leah Chen located in Columbus, Ohio, and her profile was the first one out of two that popped up. She went to Miami University to study psychology and then to Ohio State shortly after for what I'm assuming was for her master's degree. The profile picture was a picture of one of those crusty-eyed white dogs being taken on a walk.

12

Giovanni is having a panic attack on the phone. The police are at his door and he is hiding in the basement. He's breathing heavily and crying. I just know there is hella snot slipping down his nose.

"Athena, please. I'm sorry for what I did."

"I don't think you are," I respond calmly.

"Yes, I am. I'm sorry." His crying gets louder.

"What are you sorry for?" I play dumb.

"I'm sorry for doing that awful stuff. I'm sorry, I'll stop doing it! I'm sorry for everything. The controlling, the embarrassing you, and the hitting."

"Giovanni, I forgive you. But this is the end of us. Goodbye."

"What?" He stops crying, sounding confused.

I can hear the police suddenly storm into the basement room he is in and grab him. I end the call, looking around the room. I start giggling uncontrollably. I realize this is the end for me and something big has been lifted off my shoulders.

13

I assumed everything in my life was all taken care of, but it got worse at 1:00 a.m. Makena, Amina, Amalie, Keira, and my cousin, Ingrid, back in Germany, all messaged me at the same time.

Giovanni and Ingrid did not know each other at all but she said that Giovanni DMed her through Instagram, and that she received a video that I don't want to know about but I probably should so that it could be reported.

They told me they received a link to three different websites that showed videos of Giovanni and I being intimate.

Amalie and Makena were spam-calling me which is how I found out at 1:00 in the morning.

"I'm going to actually kill myself," I screamed and cried on the phone to Makena.

"Chill, just chill. I'm not going to let you hurt yourself," She responds calmly.

"Get fucking real Makena. Would you want to stay alive if a video of you having sex was leaked? I had no idea he had a camera recording," I say as I'm shaking.

"Athena, I'm going to report this, and this will all be taken down. I'm sure no one else besides the trusted people you know will see it."

I looked at the video and had the worst panic attack of my life. I broke my nightstand lamp, a photo frame of Mom and I back in Germany, and the empty Jack Daniels bottle. I ran into the bathroom, crying and puking.

I remember that day vividly but I was not aware of being recorded. I remember having to use the restroom before so he must have set up the camera when I was in there. I was seventeen and had platinum blonde hair. In the video, the room was dark but I'm sure someone who knows me could tell that it's me. My whole body and face are showing while you can only see the side of his body with his face being cropped out.

I don't know what to do.

— EPILOGUE —

It has been revealed that Giovanni committed two crimes in The United States: domestic violence and child pornography.

Even though Athena cuts all connections with him and blocks him, she finds out from another classmate with whom she was in a group chat that he has been deported back to Italy. With Athena being triggered hearing his name, she leaves the group chat and spends less time on her phone overall, even being on it for less than thirty minutes a day. Although she has a lot of negative emotions she is feeling, she also does feel relieved that she will never have to see him again.

When he returned to Italy, no one was happy to see him. They spit on him, called him names, and even stomped on him. His mother was angry at him and didn't want to help him at all. He was stuck living on the streets, as his uncle, too, refused to take him in. He even was so desperate that he contacted his father, but even his father didn't want him around after hearing what he did. Two weeks after he returned to Italy, his cousin was willing to let him stay at his place until he got back on his feet.

His cousin is extremely disappointed in him but decides to take him in because he understands that he is still his cousin. His cousin tries to help him find jobs but, with his criminal record, it's almost impossible. He is then introduced to a life of drugs and starts selling them. This concerns his cousin and wife, especially since they had their own kids, so his cousin then kicks him out for good.

It takes years of therapy for Athena to fully recover from what happened. Luckily, she is not recognized from the video by anyone else that she knows. The people he did send it to do not speak of it again.

Athena felt sick every time she thought of the videos so Makena decided to contact the websites they were put on and managed to get them taken down for good. Even though the videos were taken down, Athena still felt paranoid and believed that people have downloaded them and saved them for themselves. This led her to disappear from social media for a while.

A few weeks after Athena broke up with Giovanni, she made a new TikTok account just to expose Giovanni's mother's xenophobic comments on the anonymous page, and his mother ends up getting canceled. A few well-known celebrities stopped working with her and she lost over 100,000 Instagram followers. She was stressing out over it and was trying to find a way to solve the issue.

This led her to make an apology on her Instagram, but since the audience could see she was reading off of a script when her eyes shifted back and forth to the right side of the camera, they knew she was only apologizing because she got caught. She is still getting loads of backlash and has decided to disable Instagram for a while. Another reason for the temporary account disabling is because everyone knows what Giovanni did to Athena. Even though Ms. Laterza was not at fault with that situation, she felt sick from all of the comments that were questioning what Giovanni did to Athena. Giovanni's mother's followers have no idea what Athena looks like, and she is glad that her face isn't shown to the public, but she is also glad the family is being held accountable for the messed up things they did.

Athena and Dr. Chen get along really well. Athena is skeptical at first about opening up to her but after the first three therapy sessions, she becomes more specific and opens up to her about everything. Athena continues to see her for many years.

Author's Note

While attending the University of Akron, I majored in history and minored in English and sociology. I officially added sociology to my major when I was in the spring semester of my fourth year, so it was a very last-minute choice to make. I'm very grateful I chose to take these courses because they educated me on domestic violence awareness.

This may be a fictional story but there are many real-life stories like this. It is not an easy situation to escape. Throughout the novel, we see common patterns that happen to many victims of domestic violence.

Other Books by Chey Caliso

Asian Identities: Understanding Asian Americans – A short and simple non-fiction piece that focuses on Asian-American history and hearing about different perspectives of the Asian-American community.

My Filipino Parents' Worst Nightmare – A young adult fiction book that is told from 16-year-old Jaslene Dela Cruz's perspective. Her parents, mainly her mother, put her down constantly for who she is. Though this affects her mental health, she does not change who she is, which causes arguments between the two.

Black Cats Aren't Bad Luck – A children's book about a girl named Tala and her black cat, Panther. Tala is celebrating Halloween with Panther and is excited to hand out candy to the trick-or-treaters. As kids are trick-or-treating, she notices no kids in the neighborhood have come to her house. Tala and Panther have to find out why that is. The book is in English while Tagalog translations are featured below the English sentences.

Meet Kuro – A Non-fiction children's book about the life story of my ten-year-old cat, Kuro. The book is in English while Tagalog translations are featured below the English sentences.

8 Fairy Tales Coming to the Philippines – Part 1 (Mga Fairy Tales Na Darating Sa Pilipinas – Part 1) – A children's book with our favorite Western fairy tales, including Hansel and Gretel and Little Red Riding Hood, all taking place in the Philippines. The book is in English while Tagalog translations are featured below the English sentences.

Chey Around the World: Puerto Rico, California, & Oahu – A travel journal where I include budgeting for vacations, what you should pack, and places to go.